Warrior's Path to Healing:

A 12-week Empowerment Journal for Women Veterans

Kimberly Henry, LMSW
U.S. Navy Veteran

Warrior's Path to Healing: A 12-week Empowerment Journal for Women Veterans

Cover by: Kimberly Henry
Illustrated by: Kimberly Henry

ISBN: 979-8-9890549-0-9
Edition: 01

Published by: The GOLD Beacon, PLLC
PO Box 2342 San Angelo, TX 76903
www.thegoldbeacon.com

Dedication

Although my children came near the end of my military service, they have been part of my own healing. This book is a part of that healing process and for that, I dedicate this book to them.

"Thank you for your service."

Although a common term, a select few truly understand the meaning behind this sentence. Our experiences of military service vary, and we choose to define our service in our own way. But as women veterans, we are the 1.5% of American women. We have missed birthdays, holidays, and other life milestones commonly described to the general public. But as women veterans, we know there are daily sacrifices that would not otherwise be experienced if it wasn't for serving our country. Because of this and the resilience we radiate, we are invincible.

Thank you for your genuine beauty, unique identity, and underrated sacrifices.

Introduction

"Warrior's Path to Healing" journal is designed exclusively for women veterans who have faced the challenges of interpersonal violence. This carefully crafted journal serves as a compassionate companion tailored to meet each individual wherever they are on their path to recovery.

This journal becomes your confidant, assisting you in processing your trauma while respecting the uniqueness of your journey. With prompts thoughtfully structured to gradually deepen self-reflection, you will harness the power of your narrative at your own pace. As you navigate these pages, you will uncover the vast reservoirs of your resilience.

With "Warrior's Path to Healing," you will process your trauma and emerge with newfound wisdom, resilience, and a deep appreciation for your own strength. Your journey is unique, and this journal guides you every step of the way.

With love,
Kim & Daisy

Table of Contents

Self-Care

INCORPORATING THESE SELF-CARE PRACTICES INTO YOUR ROUTINE WHILE USING THE JOURNAL CAN ENHANCE YOUR HEALING JOURNEY, PROVIDING YOU WITH MOMENTS OF REST, REJUVENATION, AND PERSONAL GROWTH.

NATURE CONNECTION:
SPEND TIME OUTDOORS. NATURE CAN BE A SOOTHING BACKDROP FOR SELF-REFLECTION.

MINDFUL BREATHING:
INCORPORATE MOMENTS OF DEEP, INTENTIONAL BREATHING WHILE YOU JOURNAL.

ARTISTIC EXPRESSION:
CHANNEL YOUR EMOTIONS THROUGH CREATIVE OUTLETS LIKE DRAWING, PAINTING, OR CRAFTING.

GENTLE MOVEMENT:
ENGAGE IN GENTLE EXERCISES LIKE YOGA, STRETCHING, OR TAI CHI. MOVEMENT CAN RELEASE TENSION AND ENCOURAGE A SENSE OF WELL-BEING.

GUIDED MEDITATION:
USE GUIDED MEDITATION SESSIONS TO CENTER YOURSELF AND PROMOTE RELAXATION. THIS CAN BE ESPECIALLY HELPFUL AFTER ENGAGING WITH MORE CHALLENGING PROMPTS.

Self-Care

INCORPORATING THESE SELF-CARE PRACTICES INTO YOUR ROUTINE WHILE USING THE JOURNAL CAN ENHANCE YOUR HEALING JOURNEY, PROVIDING YOU WITH MOMENTS OF REST, REJUVENATION, AND PERSONAL GROWTH.

SOCIAL CONNECTIONS:
REACH OUT TO A TRUSTED FRIEND OR FAMILY MEMBER, FOSTERING A SENSE OF SUPPORT AND CONNECTION.

PAMPERING RITUALS:
TREAT YOURSELF TO A SMALL, HEALTHY RITUAL TO PROVIDE COMFORT AND RELAXATION.

MINDLESS READING:
DELVE INTO A BOOK OR ARTICLE THAT BRINGS YOU JOY. READING CAN OFFER AN ESCAPE AND A CHANCE TO RECHARGE.

DIGITAL DETOX:
SET ASIDE DESIGNATED TIMES TO DISCONNECT FROM SCREENS AND TECHNOLOGY. USE THESE MOMENTS TO FOCUS ON SELF-CARE AND INTROSPECTION.

DAILY REFLECTION:
TAKE A FEW MINUTES EACH DAY TO REFLECT ON YOUR JOURNALING JOURNEY. ACKNOWLEDGE YOUR PROGRESS, INSIGHTS, AND ANY SHIFTS IN YOUR EMOTIONS.

Maximizing Your Journey: Tips for Healing and Growth

CREATE A COMFORTABLE SPACE: FIND A PEACEFUL CORNER WHERE YOU CAN WRITE WITHOUT DISTRACTION, ALLOWING YOUR THOUGHTS TO FLOW FREELY.

SET A RHYTHM: DEDICATE A CONSISTENT TIME EACH DAY TO JOURNAL. ESTABLISH A ROUTINE THAT SUITS YOUR SCHEDULE, WHETHER MORNING OR NIGHT. ANSWER EACH WEEK'S PROMPTS IN ONE SITTING OR THROUGHOUT THE WEEK.

EMBRACE VULNERABILITY: LET GO OF JUDGMENT AND ALLOW YOURSELF TO EXPRESS YOUR TRUE THOUGHTS AND EMOTIONS. THIS IS YOUR PERSONAL SPACE FOR HEALING.

START WITH HONESTY: ANSWER EACH PROMPT WITH AUTHENTICITY. YOUR JOURNEY'S PROGRESS BEGINS WITH ACKNOWLEDGING WHERE YOU CURRENTLY STAND.

PROGRESS AT YOUR PACE: THIS JOURNAL IS TAILORED TO YOUR UNIQUE JOURNEY. TAKE YOUR TIME; TAKE THE TIME YOU NEED TO PROCESS EACH PROMPT.

PRACTICE SELF-CARE: REMEMBER TO CARE FOR YOUR WELL-BEING AS YOU DELVE INTO YOUR EMOTIONS. ENGAGE IN ACTIVITIES THAT BRING YOU JOY, RELAXATION, AND REJUVENATION.

USE YOUR RESOURCES: IF EMOTIONS BECOME OVERWHELMING, REACH OUT TO YOUR SUPPORT NETWORK OR A PROFESSIONAL FOR GUIDANCE AND REASSURANCE.

REFLECT AND REVISIT: AT THE END OF EACH WEEK, REFLECT ON YOUR PROGRESS. CONSIDER REVISITING EARLIER ENTRIES TO OBSERVE YOUR EVOLVING PERSPECTIVE.

Maximizing Your Journey: Tips for Healing and Growth

CELEBRATE RESILIENCE: RECOGNIZE YOUR STRENGTH AS YOU NAVIGATE THROUGH CHALLENGING PROMPTS. YOUR WILLINGNESS TO CONFRONT YOUR TRAUMA IS A TESTAMENT TO YOUR RESILIENCE.

PRACTICE GRATITUDE: INCORPORATE MOMENTS OF GRATITUDE IN YOUR ENTRIES. FOCUSING ON THE POSITIVE ASPECTS OF YOUR LIFE CAN ENHANCE YOUR HEALING JOURNEY.

SET BOUNDARIES: RESPECT YOUR EMOTIONAL CAPACITY. IF YOU'RE FEELING OVERWHELMED, TAKE A BREAK AND RETURN TO YOUR JOURNAL WHEN READY. IF A PROMPT FEELS TOO CHALLENGING OR TRIGGERING, IT'S OKAY TO SKIP IT OR REVISIT IT LATER. YOUR COMFORT IS A PRIORITY.

EMBRACE IMPERFECTION: YOUR JOURNAL DOESN'T NEED TO BE PERFECT. EMBRACE MISTAKES AND SCRIBBLES—THEY'RE A REFLECTION OF YOUR AUTHENTIC SELF.

ENGAGE IN SELF-REFLECTION: USE THIS JOURNALING PROCESS AS AN OPPORTUNITY TO UNDERSTAND YOUR THOUGHT PATTERNS, REACTIONS, AND TRIGGERS.

STAY CURIOUS: APPROACH YOUR JOURNEY WITH AN OPEN MIND. BE CURIOUS ABOUT THE INSIGHTS AND DISCOVERIES THAT MAY EMERGE.

REMEMBER, YOUR HEALING IS A GRADUAL PROCESS, AND THIS JOURNAL IS YOUR COMPANION. BY PRACTICING SELF-CARE, HONORING YOUR EMOTIONS, AND ENGAGING WITH THE PROMPTS AUTHENTICALLY, YOU'LL UNLOCK THE FULL POTENTIAL OF "RESILIENT HEARTS" AS A TOOL FOR GROWTH AND EMPOWERMENT.

Start Here

WHY I'M HERE....

_____

_____

_____

_____

_____

_____

_____

_____

WHAT I HOPE TO GET OUT OF THIS IS....

_____

_____

_____

_____

_____

_____

_____

_____

MY PLAN TO GET THROUGH THIS JOURNAL IS TO.....

_____

_____

_____

_____

_____

_____

_____

_____

Ready?

Week 1
Your Identity
& Strength

1. REFLECT ON YOUR DECISION TO JOIN THE MILITARY AS A WOMAN. WHAT MOTIVATED YOU? HOW HAVE YOUR MOTIVATIONS EVOLVED?

_____

_____

_____

_____

_____

_____

_____

_____

_____

_____

_____

_____

_____

_____

_____

_____

_____

_____

_____

_____

Week 1
Your Identity & Strength

2. DESCRIBE A TIME WHEN YOU FELT PROUD OF YOUR ACHIEVEMENTS AS A WOMAN IN THE MILITARY.

_____

_____

_____

_____

_____

_____

_____

_____

_____

_____

_____

_____

_____

_____

_____

_____

_____

_____

_____

_____

Week 1
Your Identity
& Strength

3. SHARE AN EXPERIENCE WHEN YOUR RESILIENCE AS A WOMAN IN THE MILITARY WAS TESTED. HOW DID YOU OVERCOME IT?

_____

_____

_____

_____

_____

_____

_____

_____

_____

_____

_____

_____

_____

_____

_____

_____

_____

_____

_____

_____

_____

This week's affirmation:

I am a woman of strength and purpose, empowered by my unique journey.

Reflections

I AM PROUD OF:

_____

_____

_____

_____

_____

_____

I AM GRATEFUL FOR:

_____

_____

_____

_____

_____

_____

SUCCESS FROM THIS WEEK:

_____

_____

_____

_____

_____

_____

Thoughts, Goals, Doodles, & Notes

Week 2
Challenging &
Overcoming Norms

1. WHAT NORMS DO YOU BELIEVE ARE UNIQUE TO THE MILITARY ENVIRONMENT?

_____

_____

_____

_____

_____

_____

_____

_____

_____

_____

_____

_____

_____

_____

_____

_____

_____

_____

_____

_____

_____

Week 2
Challenging & Overcoming Norms

2. DESCRIBE A MOMENT WHEN YOU FACED ADVERSITY
BASED ON YOUR GENDER. HOW DID YOU RISE ABOVE IT?

_____

_____

_____

_____

_____

_____

_____

_____

_____

_____

_____

_____

_____

_____

_____

_____

_____

_____

_____

Week 2
Challenging &
Overcoming Norms

3. WHAT STRENGTHS DO YOU BELIEVE WOMEN BRING TO THE MILITARY?

_____

_____

_____

_____

_____

_____

_____

_____

_____

_____

_____

_____

_____

_____

_____

_____

_____

_____

_____

This week's
affirmation:

I break barriers,
challenge norms, and
rise above adversity
with grace.

Reflections

I AM PROUD OF:

_____

_____

_____

_____

_____

_____

I AM GRATEFUL FOR:

_____

_____

_____

_____

_____

_____

SUCCESS FROM THIS WEEK:

_____

_____

_____

_____

_____

_____

Thoughts, Goals, Doodles, & Notes

Week 3
Trauma & Triumph

1. WHAT DOES TRAUMA MEAN TO YOU?

_____

_____

_____

_____

_____

_____

_____

_____

_____

_____

_____

_____

_____

_____

_____

_____

_____

_____

_____

_____

_____

_____

Week 3
Trauma & Triumph

2. RECALL A TRAUMATIC INCIDENT THAT YOU'VE HELD ONTO. WRITE DOWN THE KEY DETAILS.

_____

_____

_____

_____

_____

_____

_____

_____

_____

_____

_____

_____

_____

_____

_____

_____

_____

_____

_____

_____

_____

_____

_____

Week 3
Trauma & Triumph

3. REFLECT ON THE RESILIENCE THAT CARRIED YOU
THROUGH TRAUMATIC MOMENTS.
HOW HAS IT SHAPED YOUR STRENGTH TODAY?

_____

_____

_____

_____

_____

_____

_____

_____

_____

_____

_____

_____

_____

_____

_____

_____

_____

_____

_____

_____

This week's affirmation:

I honor my resilience as I heal from past traumas, embracing my triumphs.

Reflections

I AM PROUD OF:

_____

_____

_____

_____

_____

_____

I AM GRATEFUL FOR:

_____

_____

_____

_____

_____

_____

SUCCESS FROM THIS WEEK:

_____

_____

_____

_____

_____

Thoughts, Goals, Doodles, & Notes

Week 4
Embracing Transformation

1. DESCRIBE YOUR EMOTIONAL LANDSCAPE AS A WOMAN IN THE MILITARY. HOW CAN UNDERSTANDING THESE EMOTIONS AID IN YOUR HEALING?

_____

_____

_____

_____

_____

_____

_____

_____

_____

_____

_____

_____

_____

_____

_____

_____

_____

_____

_____

_____

_____

_____

Week 4
Embracing Transformation

2. REFLECT ON A MOMENT WHEN YOU FOUND STRENGTH IN VULNERABILITY WHILE SERVING. HOW HAS THIS IMPACTED YOUR GROWTH?

_____

_____

_____

_____

_____

_____

_____

_____

_____

_____

_____

_____

_____

_____

_____

_____

_____

_____

Week 4
Embracing Transformation

3. WRITE ABOUT EMOTIONS THAT YOU'RE READY TO RELEASE, AND THOSE YOU WANT TO CULTIVATE ON YOUR JOURNEY TO HEALING.

_____

_____

_____

_____

_____

_____

_____

_____

_____

_____

_____

_____

_____

_____

_____

_____

_____

_____

_____

_____

_____

This week's
affirmation:

I embrace my
emotions as tools for
transformation and
growth.

Reflections

I AM PROUD OF:

_____

_____

_____

_____

_____

_____

I AM GRATEFUL FOR:

_____

_____

_____

_____

_____

_____

SUCCESS FROM THIS WEEK:

_____

_____

_____

_____

_____

_____

Thoughts, Goals, Doodles, & Notes

Week 5
Advocacy & Empowerment

1. DESCRIBE A MOMENT WHEN YOU LEANED ON THE SUPPORT OF OTHER WOMEN VETERANS TO NAVIGATE TRAUMA. HOW DID THIS SOLIDARITY IMPACT YOUR HEALING?

_____

_____

_____

_____

_____

_____

_____

_____

_____

_____

_____

_____

_____

_____

_____

_____

_____

_____

Week 5
Advocacy &
Empowerment

2. WRITE ABOUT THE MENTORS WHO GUIDED YOU AS A
WOMAN IN THE MILITARY. HOW HAVE THEIR LESSONS
INFLUENCED YOUR HEALING JOURNEY?

_____

_____

_____

_____

_____

_____

_____

_____

_____

_____

_____

_____

_____

_____

_____

_____

_____

_____

_____

_____

Week 5
Advocacy &
Empowerment

3. SHARE HOW EMPOWERING OTHER WOMEN IN THE MILITARY
HAS EMPOWERED YOU IN RETURN.

_____

_____

_____

_____

_____

_____

_____

_____

_____

_____

_____

_____

_____

_____

_____

_____

_____

_____

_____

_____

_____

This week's
affirmation:

I use my voice to
advocate for change
and empower those
around me.

Reflections

I AM PROUD OF:

_____
_____
_____
_____
_____
_____

I AM GRATEFUL FOR:

_____
_____
_____
_____
_____
_____

SUCCESS FROM THIS WEEK:

_____
_____
_____
_____
_____
_____

Thoughts, Goals, Doodles, & Notes

Week 6
Reclaiming Identity

1. HOW HAS BECOMING A VETERAN IMPACTED YOUR TRAUMATIC EXPERIENCES?

_____

_____

_____

_____

_____

_____

_____

_____

_____

_____

_____

_____

_____

_____

_____

_____

_____

_____

_____

_____

_____

_____

_____

_____

_____

_____

Week 6
Reclaiming Identity

2. AS A VETERAN, HOW DO YOU DEFINE YOUR MILITARY SERVICE?

_____

_____

_____

_____

_____

_____

_____

_____

_____

_____

_____

_____

_____

_____

_____

_____

_____

_____

_____

_____

_____

_____

_____

Week 6
Reclaiming Identity

3. REFLECT ON HOW YOU'VE RETAINED YOUR IDENTITY AS A WOMAN VETERAN WHILE EMBRACING NEW OPPORTUNITIES.

_____

_____

_____

_____

_____

_____

_____

_____

_____

_____

_____

_____

_____

_____

_____

_____

_____

_____

_____

_____

_____

_____

_____

This week's
affirmation:

I transition with
courage, embracing
new opportunities
while honoring my
identity.

Reflections

I AM PROUD OF:

_____

_____

_____

_____

_____

_____

I AM GRATEFUL FOR:

_____

_____

_____

_____

_____

_____

SUCCESS FROM THIS WEEK:

_____

_____

_____

_____

_____

_____

Thoughts, Goals, Doodles, & Notes

Week 7
Self-Compassion & Reconciliation

1. WRITE A LETTER OF COMPASSION TO YOURSELF, ACKNOWLEDGING YOUR FAVORITE TRAITS.

_____
_____
_____
_____
_____
_____
_____
_____
_____
_____
_____
_____
_____
_____
_____
_____
_____
_____
_____
_____
_____
_____

Week 7
Self-Compassion & Reconciliation

2. SHARE HOW YOU'VE RECONCILED ANY CONFLICTS BETWEEN YOUR MILITARY IDENTITY AND YOUR CIVILIAN IDENTITY.

_____

_____

_____

_____

_____

_____

_____

_____

_____

_____

_____

_____

_____

_____

_____

_____

_____

_____

_____

_____

Week 7
Self-Compassion & Reconciliation

3. DEFINE SELF COMPASSION. HOW WILL YOU PRACTICE IT MORE IN YOUR DAILY LIFE?

_____

_____

_____

_____

_____

_____

_____

_____

_____

_____

_____

_____

_____

_____

_____

_____

_____

_____

_____

_____

_____

_____

This week's affirmation:

I reflect on my journey, reconciling the past as I step into my future.

Reflections

I AM PROUD OF:

_____

_____

_____

_____

_____

_____

I AM GRATEFUL FOR:

_____

_____

_____

_____

_____

_____

SUCCESS FROM THIS WEEK:

_____

_____

_____

_____

_____

_____

Thoughts, Goals, Doodles, & Notes

Week 8
Navigating Trauma's Impact

1. HOW CAN YOU ACKNOWLEDGE YOUR TRAUMA WITHOUT INVALIDATING YOUR FEELINGS?

_____

_____

_____

_____

_____

_____

_____

_____

_____

_____

_____

_____

_____

_____

_____

_____

_____

_____

_____

_____

_____

Week 8
Navigating Trauma's Impact

2. DESCRIBE A PIVOTAL MOMENT DURING YOUR MILITARY SERVICE THAT SHAPED YOUR PERSPECTIVE ON HEALING AND RESILIENCE.

_____

_____

_____

_____

_____

_____

_____

_____

_____

_____

_____

_____

_____

_____

_____

_____

_____

_____

_____

_____

Week 8
Navigating Trauma's Impact

3. WHAT DOES LETTING GO OF TRAUMA LOOK LIKE FOR YOU? WHAT CAN YOU DO TO GET TO THAT POINT?

_____

_____

_____

_____

_____

_____

_____

_____

_____

_____

_____

_____

_____

_____

_____

_____

_____

_____

_____

_____

_____

This week's affirmation:

My journey is my own to define.

Reflections

I AM PROUD OF:

_____
_____
_____
_____
_____
_____

I AM GRATEFUL FOR:

_____
_____
_____
_____
_____
_____

SUCCESS FROM THIS WEEK:

_____
_____
_____
_____
_____
_____

Thoughts, Goals, Doodles, & Notes

Week 9
Recognizing Resilience

1. HOW DO YOU DEFINE RESILIENCE?

_____

_____

_____

_____

_____

_____

_____

_____

_____

_____

_____

_____

_____

_____

_____

_____

_____

_____

_____

_____

Week 9
Recognizing Resilience

2. DESCRIBE WHAT MAKES YOU RESILIENT. DO YOU BELIEVE THAT BEING TOLD YOU'RE RESILIENT IS A COMPLIMENT?

_____

_____

_____

_____

_____

_____

_____

_____

_____

_____

_____

_____

_____

_____

_____

_____

_____

_____

_____

_____

_____

_____

Week 9
Recognizing Resilience

3. WRITE ABOUT THE UNIQUE WAYS IN WHICH YOUR EXPERIENCES AS A WOMAN IN THE MILITARY HAVE SHAPED YOUR DEFINITION OF RESILIENCE.

_____

_____

_____

_____

_____

_____

_____

_____

_____

_____

_____

_____

_____

_____

_____

_____

_____

_____

_____

_____

_____

_____

This week's affirmation:

Resilience doesn't mean never again having a rough day. I'm human.

Reflections

I AM PROUD OF:

_____
_____
_____
_____
_____
_____

I AM GRATEFUL FOR:

_____
_____
_____
_____
_____
_____

SUCCESS FROM THIS WEEK:

_____
_____
_____
_____
_____

Thoughts, Goals, Doodles, & Notes

Week 10
Building Connections

1. DESCRIBE THE CAMARADERIE YOU EXPERIENCED WITH FELLOW WOMEN IN THE MILITARY. HOW DID THESE CONNECTIONS SHAPE YOUR JOURNEY?

_____

_____

_____

_____

_____

_____

_____

_____

_____

_____

_____

_____

_____

_____

_____

_____

_____

_____

_____

_____

_____

Week 10
Building Connections

2. HOW DOES TELLING YOUR STORY TO OTHERS BUILD YOUR CONNECTEDNESS WITH THEM?

_____

_____

_____

_____

_____

_____

_____

_____

_____

_____

_____

_____

_____

_____

_____

_____

_____

_____

_____

_____

_____

_____

_____

Week 10
Building Connections

3. REFLECT ON HOW SHARING YOUR EXPERIENCES WITH OTHERS HAS CONTRIBUTED TO YOUR GROWTH AND HEALING.

_____

_____

_____

_____

_____

_____

_____

_____

_____

_____

_____

_____

_____

_____

_____

_____

_____

_____

_____

_____

This week's
affirmation:

I am worthy of being
heard and celebrated.

Reflections

I AM PROUD OF:

_____

_____

_____

_____

_____

_____

I AM GRATEFUL FOR:

_____

_____

_____

_____

_____

_____

SUCCESS FROM THIS WEEK:

_____

_____

_____

_____

_____

_____

Thoughts, Goals, Doodles, & Notes

Week 11
Shared
Empowerment

1. WRITE A LETTER TO YOUR YOUNGER SELF, OFFERING STRENGTH AND GUIDANCE AS A WOMAN ENTERING THE MILITARY.

_____

_____

_____

_____

_____

_____

_____

_____

_____

_____

_____

_____

_____

_____

_____

_____

_____

_____

_____

_____

Week 11
Shared
Empowerment

2. REFLECT ON THE LEGACY YOU WANT TO LEAVE FOR
FUTURE GENERATIONS OF WOMEN IN THE MILITARY.

_____

_____

_____

_____

_____

_____

_____

_____

_____

_____

_____

_____

_____

_____

_____

_____

_____

_____

_____

_____

_____

_____

Week 11
Shared Empowerment

3. REFLECT ON HOW YOUR STORY CAN INSPIRE FELLOW WOMEN VETERANS TO FIND EMPOWERMENT AND RESILIENCE.

_____

_____

_____

_____

_____

_____

_____

_____

_____

_____

_____

_____

_____

_____

_____

_____

_____

_____

_____

This week's affirmation:

I shape my legacy by inspiring future generations with my strength and wisdom.

Reflections

I AM PROUD OF:

_____

_____

_____

_____

_____

_____

I AM GRATEFUL FOR:

_____

_____

_____

_____

_____

_____

SUCCESS FROM THIS WEEK:

_____

_____

_____

_____

_____

_____

Thoughts, Goals, Doodles, & Notes

Week 12
Looking Forward

1. REFLECT ON THE PROGRESS YOU'VE MADE THROUGHOUT THIS JOURNAL. HOW HAVE YOU EVOLVED?

_____

_____

_____

_____

_____

_____

_____

_____

_____

_____

_____

_____

_____

_____

_____

_____

_____

_____

_____

_____

_____

_____

_____

Week 12
Looking Forward

2. WRITE ABOUT HOW YOU'LL CONTINUE TO HONOR YOUR
EXPERIENCES AS YOU MOVE FORWARD.

_____

_____

_____

_____

_____

_____

_____

_____

_____

_____

_____

_____

_____

_____

_____

_____

_____

_____

_____

_____

_____

_____

Week 12
Looking Forward

3. WRITE A LETTER OF APPRECIATION AND RESPECT TO YOURSELF FOR COMPLETING THIS JOURNAL.

_____

_____

_____

_____

_____

_____

_____

_____

_____

_____

_____

_____

_____

_____

_____

_____

_____

_____

_____

_____

_____

_____

_____

This week's affirmation:

I celebrate my journey, embracing the empowered woman I've become as I move forward.

Reflections

I AM PROUD OF:

_____

_____

_____

_____

_____

_____

I AM GRATEFUL FOR:

_____

_____

_____

_____

_____

_____

SUCCESS FROM THIS WEEK:

_____

_____

_____

_____

_____

Thoughts, Goals, Doodles, & Notes

Resources

NEVER HESITATE TO REACH OUT FOR HELP.
THIS WORLD NEEDS YOU.
HERE ARE SOME OF OUR FAVORITE RESOURCES.

GLASSSOLDIER.ORG

WOMENVETERANSALLIANCE.COM

CALL 988
VETERANS PRESS 1
TEXT 838255

CALL 800.799.7233
TEXT "START" 88788
TTY 800.787.3224

 **LGBT National Help Center**

888.843.4564

Breathe & Celebrate

AS YOU REACH THE FINAL PAGES OF THIS TRANSFORMATIVE JOURNALING JOURNEY, REMEMBER THAT HEALING IS NOT A LINEAR PATH; IT'S A COURAGEOUS EXPLORATION OF YOUR INNER LANDSCAPE. YOU'VE DELVED DEEP, UNCOVERING EMOTIONS, TRUTHS, AND STRENGTHS YOU MIGHT NOT HAVE REALIZED WERE THERE. THIS PROCESS IS A TESTAMENT TO YOUR RESILIENCE; YOU DESERVE EVERY OUNCE OF CREDIT FOR YOUR PROGRESS.

AS YOU CLOSE THIS CHAPTER, I ENCOURAGE YOU TO TAKE THESE LESSONS AND REVELATIONS INTO YOUR DAILY LIFE. PRACTICE THE HEALTHY COPING MECHANISMS YOU'VE IDENTIFIED, AND EXTEND THE SAME COMPASSION TO YOURSELF THAT YOU'VE SHARED ON THESE PAGES. REMEMBER THAT SELF-CARE IS NOT SELFISH; IT'S VITAL TO YOUR ONGOING WELL-BEING.

KNOW THAT YOUR JOURNEY DOESN'T END HERE. WHEN THE TIME IS RIGHT, CONSIDER REVISITING THESE PROMPTS. JUST AS THE SEASONS CHANGE, SO DO OUR EMOTIONS AND PERSPECTIVES. REENGAGING WITH THIS PROCESS CAN HELP YOU UNCOVER NEW LAYERS OF UNDERSTANDING, GROWTH, AND HEALING. YOUR STORY IS EVOLVING, AND YOU HOLD THE PEN.

MAY YOU NURTURE YOUR SPIRIT, CULTIVATE SELF-LOVE, AND EMBRACE THE JOURNEY AHEAD WITH GRACE AND COURAGE. YOU ARE STRONG, RESILIENT, AND WORTHY OF THE ABUNDANT LIFE THAT AWAITS YOU.

Notes

Notes

We want to hear from you.

Please consider leaving a review on the retailer platform in which you purchased this journal.

Thank you.